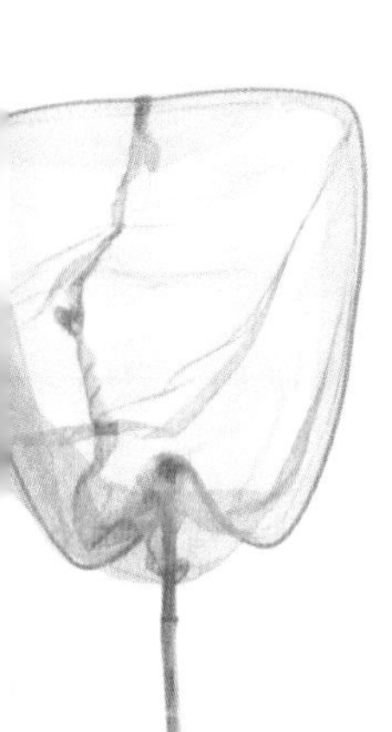

Sarah Hatton Knits...

10 simple, cosy projects.

Sarah Hatton

First published in Great Britain in 2011 by
Daco Technology Ltd.
www.dacotechnology.co.uk

Second Edition printed in 2011

ISBN 978-0-9567851-0-7

Simple Snug Scarf

Cherish Scarf

Super Stripes Scarf

Simple Snug Hat

Nuzzle Hat

His & Hers Sweater

Nuzzle Scarf

Toasty Wristwarmers

Cosy Classic Sweater

His & Hers Sweater

Nestle Headband

Location, Location! Walberswick
Was it this way?
Toasted marshmallows on an open fire...
At last, a chance to rest!

fishing
I must get this scarf finished!
FERRY HOUSE
Writing home
Shall we go for lunch?

Simple Snug Scarf

YARN USED
Rowan Big Wool
4 x 100gm balls (shown in Linen 048)
Each ball will work approx 50cm/19½in of scarf.
I made mine 210cm/83in.

NEEDLES
1 pair 10mm (US 15) needles

Scarf:
Make a Slip knot and cast on 22 stitches.
Row 1: Knit every stitch.
Repeat this row until scarf reaches desired length.
Cast off.
Sew in ends.
At this point you may want to add fringing to the ends of your scarf.

Cherish Scarf

YARN USED
Rowan Big Wool
3 x 100gm balls (shown in Smoky 007)
Each ball will work approx 60cm/23½in of scarf.
I made mine 170cm/67in long.

NEEDLES
1 pair 10mm (US 15) needles

Scarf:
Make a Slip knot and cast on 27 stitches.
Row 1: Knit every stitch.
Row 2: Purl every stitch.
These 2 rows set stocking stitch.
Continue in stocking stitch working rows 1 and 2 until scarf reaches desired length.
Cast off.
At this point you may also wish to join the ends to form a loop scarf.

Super Stripes Scarf

YARN USED
Rowan Big Wool
Shade A – 2 x 100gm (Blue Velvet 026)
Shade B – 1 x 100gm (Zing 037)
Shade C – 1 x 100gm (Glamour 036)
Shade D – 1 x 100gm (Heather 058)

NEEDLES
1 pair 10mm (US 15) needles

Scarf:
Make a Slip knot and cast on 23 stitches.
Working in stocking stitch (1 row knit, 1 row purl) throughout, work in stripe pattern as set below until scarf measures 258cm/101½ in, or desired length, ending with right side facing for next row.
Cast off.

Stripe pattern
Work 10 rows in A.
Work 4 rows in B.
Work 2 rows in A.
Work 2 rows in C.
Work 6 rows in D.
Work 2 rows in B.
Work 2 rows in D.
Work 4 rows in A.
Work 4 rows in C.
Work 2 rows in B.

Simple Snug Hat

YARN USED
Rowan Big Wool
1 x 100gm ball (shown in Smoky 007)

NEEDLES
1 pair 10mm (US 15) needles

Hat:
Make a Slip knot and cast on
41 stitches.
Row 1: Knit all stitches.
Row 2 : Purl all stitches.
Repeat the last 2 rows until work measures 16cm/6½in, ending with right side facing for next row.
Shape crown.
Next row: (Knit 6, knit 2 stitches together) 5 times, knit 1. (36 stitches)
Next row: Purl.
Next row: (Knit 5, knit 2 stitches together) 5 times, knit 1. (31 stitches)
Next row: Purl.
Next row: (Knit 4, knit 2 stitches together) 5 times, knit 1. (26 stitches)
Next row: Purl 1, (purl 2 stitches together, purl 3) 5 times. (21 stitches)
Next row: (Knit 2, knit 2 stitches together) 5 times, knit 1. (16 stitches)
Next row: Purl 1, (purl 2 stitches together, purl 1) 5 times. (11 stitches)
Next row: (Knit 2 stitches together) 5 times, knit 1. (6 stitches)
Break yarn and thread through the remaining stitches.
Fasten off.

Using mattress stitch join back seam

Nuzzle Hat

YARN USED
Rowan Cocoon
1 x 100g (shown in Tundra 808)

NEEDLES
1 pair 7mm (US 10½) needles.

Hat:
Make a Slip knot and cast on 74 stitches.
Working in 2 x 2 rib as follows:
Row 1: Knit 2, * purl 2, knit 2, repeat from * to end.

Row 2: * Purl 2, knit 2, repeat from * to last 2 stitches, purl 2.
These 2 rows set rib.
Work 6 rows more in rib.

Next row: Knit 2 together, knit to end. 73 stitches.
Beginning with a purl row, work in stocking stitch until work measures 17cm/6 ½in, ending with right side facing for next row.

Shape crown
Next row: (Knit 7, knit 2 together) 8 times, knit 1. 65 stitches.
Next row: Purl.
Next row: Knit.
Next row: Purl.
Next row: (Knit 6, knit 2 together) 8 times, knit 1. 57 stitches.
Next row: Purl.
Next row: (Knit 5, knit 2 together) 8 times, knit 1. 49 stitches.
Next row: Purl.
Next row: (Knit 4, knit 2 together) 8 times, knit 1. 41 stitches.
Next row: Purl.
Next row: (Knit 3, knit 2 together) 8 times, knit 1. 33 stitches.
Next row: Purl.
Next row: (Knit 2, knit 2 together) 8 times, knit 1. 25 stitches.
Next row: Purl 1, (purl 2 together) 12 times. 13 stitches.
Next row: (Knit 2 together) 6 times, knit 1. 7 stitches.
Break yarn and thread through the remaining stitches.
Fasten off.

Using mattress stitch join back seam.

Nuzzle Scarf

YARN USED
Rowan Cocoon
4 x 100gm balls (shown in Tundra 808)
Each ball will work approx 80cm/31½in of scarf.
I made mine 330cm/130in long

NEEDLES
1 pair 7mm (US 10½) needles.

Scarf:
Make a Slip knot and cast on 30 stitches.
Working in 2 x 2 rib as follows:
Row 1: Knit 2, * purl 2, knit 2, repeat from * to end.
Row 2: * Purl 2, knit 2, repeat from * to last 2 stitches, purl 2.
These 2 rows set the 2 x 2 rib.
Continue in rib until scarf measures desired length.
Cast off in rib.
Sew in ends.

Toasty Wristwarmers

YARN USED
Rowan Cocoon
1 x 100gm (shown in Seascape 813)

NEEDLES
1 pair 6½mm (US 10½) needles

Wristwarmers:
Make a Slip knot and cast on 27 stitches.
Work in Single rib as follows:
Row 1: Knit 1, * purl 1, knit 1, repeat from * to end.
Row 2: * Purl 1, knit 1, repeat from * to last stitch, purl 1.
These 2 rows set rib.
Continue in rib until wristwarmers reach desired length
(I have made mine 21cm/8½in).
Cast off in rib.

Using mattress stitch, join seam for approx 4cm/1½in (this will form the part that wraps around your hand, leave a gap of approx 4cm/1½in (for thumb) then join the remaining part of the seam.
Finish second wristwarmer to match.

Cosy Classic Sweater

To fit

S	M	L
32-34	36-38	40-42
81-86	92-97	101-107

XL	XXL	
44-46	48-50	in
112-117	122-127	cm

Actual Measurements
Width (laid flat) 44 [51:55:62:69]cm (17½ [20:21½ :24½:27¼]in)
Length 52 [54:56:58:60]cm (20½ [21½:22:22¾:23¾]in)
Sleeve length 45 [46:47:47:47]cm (17½ [18:18½:18½:18½]in)

YARN USED
Rowan Kid Classic
6 [6:7:7:8] x 50gm balls
(shown in Peat 832)

NEEDLES
1 pair 4mm (US 6) needles
1 pair 5mm (US 8) needles

TENSION
19 stitches and 25 rows to 10cm/4in measured over stocking stitch on 5mm needles.

BACK
Using 4mm needles cast on 86 [98:104:118:130] stitches.
Working in 2x2 rib as follows;
Row 1 (RS): Knit 2, * purl 2, knit 2, repeat from * to end.
Row 2: * Purl 2, knit 2, repeat from * to last 2 stitches, purl 2.
These 2 rows set rib.
Work 7 [7:8:8:8]cm/3in in rib, ending with right side facing for next row.
Change to 5mm needles and beginning with a knit row, continue in stocking stitch until back measures 31 [32:33:34:35]cm/ 12[12½:13:13½:13¾]in, ending with right side facing for next row.

Shape armholes
Decrease 1 stitch at each end of next 7 [9:11:13:15] rows. 72 [80:82:92:100] stitches.
Continue without shaping until armhole measures 20 [21:22:23:24]cm/ 8 [8½:8¾:9:9½]in, ending with right side facing for next row.
Shape shoulders
Cast off 9 [11:11:14:15] stitches at beginning of next 2 rows.
54 [58:60:64:70] stitches.
Cast off 10 [12:12:14:16] stitches at beginning of next 2 rows.
34 [34:36:36:38] stitches.
Cast off remaining stitches.

FRONT

Work as given for Back until armhole measures 12 [13:13:14:14]cm/ 4½ [5:5:5½:5½]in, ending with right side facing for next row.

Shape front neck

Next row: Knit 29 [33:34:39:42], turn and leave remaining stitches on a holder.

Work 1 row.

Decrease 1 stitch at neck edge in next 7 [7:7:5:5] rows, then on 3 [3:4:6:6] following alternate rows. 19 [23:23:28:31] stitches.

Continue without shaping until armhole measures 20 [21:22:23:24]cm/ 8 [8½:8¾:9:9½]in, ending with right side facing for next row.

Shape shoulder

Next row: Cast off 9 [11:11:14:15] stitches at beginning of row. 10 [12:12:14:16] stitches.

Work 1 row.

Cast off remaining 10 [12:12:14:16] stitches.

With right side facing, working on remaining stitches, cast off centre 14 [14:14:14:16] stitches, knit to end.

Work 1 row.

Decrease 1 stitch at neck edge in next 7 [7:7:5:5] rows, then on 3 [3:4:6:6] following alternate rows. 19 [23:23:28:31] stitches.

Continue without shaping until armhole measures 20 [21:22:23:24]cm/ 8 [8½:8¾:9:9½]in, ending with wrong side facing for next row.

Shape shoulder

Next row: Cast off 9 [11:11:14:15] stitches at beginning of row. 10 [12:12:14:16] stitches remain.

Work 1 row.

Cast off remaining 10 [12:12:14:16] stitches.

SLEEVES (Both alike)

Using 4mm needles cast on 42 [46:50:50:54] stitches.

Row 1 (RS): Knit 2, * purl 2, knit 2, repeat from * to end.

Row 2: * Purl 2, knit 2, repeat from * to last 2 stitches, purl 2.

These 2 rows set rib.

Work in rib for 6 [6:7:7:7]cm / 2½ [2½:3:3:3]in, ending with right side of next row.

Change to 5mm needles and beginning with a knit row, working in stocking stitch continue as follows:-

Increase 1 stitch at each end of next and 9 [3:4:4:4] following 8th [8th:8th:6th:6th] rows, then on every following 10th [10th:10th:8th:8th] row to 64 [66:70:74:78] stitches.

Continue without shaping until sleeve measures 45 [46:47:47:47]cm/ 17½ [18:18½:18½:18½]in, or length required, ending with right side facing for next row.

Shape sleeve top

Decrease 1 stitch at each end of next 7 [9:11:13:15] rows. 50 [48:48:48:48] stitches.

Cast off remaining 50 [48:48:48:48] stitches.

MAKING UP

Join right shoulder seam.

NECKBAND

With right side facing, using 4mm needles pick up and knit 20 [20:22:22:24] stitches down left side of neck, pick up and knit 14 [14:14:14:16] stitches from front neck, pick up and knit 20 [20:22:22:24] stitches up right side of neck and pick up and knit 34 [34:36:36:38] stitches from back neck. 90 [90:94:94:102] stitches.

Row 1 (Wrong side): Purl 2, * knit 2, purl 2, repeat from * to end.

Row 2: * Knit 2, purl 2, repeat from * to last 2 stitches, knit 2.

These 2 rows set rib.

Work in rib until neckband measures 7cm/3in, ending with right side facing for next row.

Cast off in rib.

His & Hers Sweater

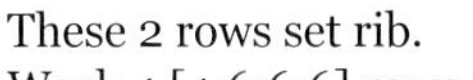

To fit

S	M	L
32-34	36-38	40-42
81-86	92-97	101-107

XL	XXL	
44-46	48-50	in
112-117	122-127	cm

Actual Measurements (laid flat)
Width 53 [58:63:69:76]cm
(21 [23:25:27¼:30]in)
Length 63 [65:67:69:71]cm
(25 [25½:26½:27¼:28]in)
Sleeve length 47 [48:49:49:49]cm
(18½[19:19½:19½:19½]in)

YARN USED
Rowan Cocoon
7 [7:8:9:10] x 100gm balls (shown in Crag 809)

NEEDLES
1 pair 6mm (10) needles
1 pair 7mm (10½) needles

TENSION
14 stitches and 19 rows to 10cm measured over stocking stitch on 7mm needles.

BACK
Using 6mm needles cast on 75 [81:89:97:107] stitches.
Working in Single rib as follows:
Row 1 (RS): Knit 1, * purl 1, knit 1, repeat from * to end.
Row 2: * Purl 1, knit 1, repeat from * to last stitch, purl 1.
These 2 rows set rib.
Work 4 [4:6:6:6] rows more in rib, ending with right side facing for next row.
Change to 7mm needles and beginning with a knit row, continue in stocking stitch until back measures 40 [41:42:43:44]cm/ 15½[16:16½:17:17¼]in, ending with right side facing for next row.
Shape armholes
Decrease 1 stitch at each end of next 3 [5:5:7:7] rows. 69 [71:79:83:93] stitches.
Continue without shaping until armhole measures 22 [23:24:25:26]cm/ 8½[9:9½:9¾:10¼]in, ending with right side facing for next row.
Shape shoulders
Cast off 10 [11:12:13:15] stitches at beginning of next 2 rows.
49 [49:55:57:63] stitches.
Cast off 11 [11:13:14:16] stitches at beginning of next 2 rows.
27 [27:29:29:31] stitches.
Cast off remaining stitches.

FRONT
Work as given for Back until armhole measures 16 [17:17:18:18]cm/

6½[6¾:6¾:7:7]in, ending with right side facing for next row.

Shape front neck

Next row: Knit 26 [27:31:33:37], turn and leave remaining stitches on a holder.

Work 1 row.

Decrease 1 stitch at neck edge in next 5 [5:6:6:5] rows, then on 0 [0:0:0:1] following alternate row.

21 [22:25:27:31] stitches.

Continue without shaping until armhole measures 22 [23:24:25:26]cm/ 8½[9:9½:9¾:10¼]in, ending with right side facing for next row.

Shape shoulder

Next row: Cast off 10 [11:12:13:15] stitches at beginning of row.

11 [11:13:14:16] stitches.

Work 1 row.

Cast off remaining 11 [11:13:14:16] stitches.

With right side facing, working on remaining stitches, cast off centre 17 [17:17:17:19] stitches, knit to end.

Work 1 row.

Decrease 1 stitch at neck edge in next 5 [5:6:6:5] rows, then on 0 [0:0:0:1] following alternate row.

21 [22:25:27:31] stitches.

Continue without shaping until armhole measures 22 [23:24:25:26]cm/ 8½[9:9½:9¾:10¼]in, ending with wrong side facing for next row.

Shape shoulder

Next row: Cast off 10 [11:12:13:15] stitches at beginning of row.

11 [11:13:14:16] stitches.

Work 1 row.

Cast off remaining 11 [11:13:14:16] stitches.

SLEEVES (Both alike)

Using 6mm needles cast on 31 [33:35:35:37] stitches.

Row 1 (RS): Knit 1, * purl 1, knit 1, repeat from * to end.

Row 2: * Purl 1, knit 1, repeat from * to last stitch, purl 1.

These 2 rows set rib.

Work in rib for 4 rows, ending with right side of next row.

Change to 7mm needles and beginning with a knit row, working in stocking stitch continue as follows:-

Increase 1 stitch at each end of 5th and 3 [2:1:8:10] following 6th rows, then on every following 8th row to 49 [51:55:59:63] stitches.

Continue without shaping until sleeve measures 47 [48:49:49:49]cm/ 18½ [19;19½:19½:19½]in, or length required, ending with right side facing for next row.

Shape sleeve top

Decrease 1 stitch at each end of next 3 [5:5:7:7] rows. 43 [41:45:45:49] stitches.

Cast off remaining 43 [41:45:45:49] stitches.

MAKING UP

Join right shoulder seam.

NECKBAND

With right side facing, using 6mm needles pick up and knit 9 [9:11:11:13] stitches down left side of neck, pick up and knit 17 [17:17:17:19] stitches left on a holder at front neck, pick up and knit 10 [10:12:12:14] stitches up right side of neck and pick up and knit 27 [27:29:29:31] stitches from back neck. 63 [63:69:69:77] stitches.

Beginning with a purl row, work 5cm/2in in stocking stitch, ending with right side facing for next row.

Work 4 rows in rib as set on back.

Cast off in rib.

Nestle Headband

YARN USED
Rowan Kid Classic
(used DOUBLE throughout)
1 x 50gm ball (shown in Straw 851)

NEEDLES
1 pair 6mm (US 10) needles
Cable needle.

Split your ball of yarn in two by pulling approx half out of the centre of the ball and cut to make 2 smaller balls.
Using the two balls together, make a Slip knot and cast on 12 stitches.
Row 1: Knit.
Row 2: Knit 2, purl 8, knit 2.
Row 3: Knit 2, slip next 2 stitches onto cable needle and hold at back of work, knit 2, then knit 2 from cable needle, slip next 2 stitches onto cable needle and hold at front of work, knit 2, then knit 2 from cable needle, knit 2.
Row 4: Knit 2, purl 8, knit 2.
Row 5: Knit.
Row 6: Knit 2, purl 8, knit 2.
Row 7: Knit 2, slip next 2 stitches onto cable needle and hold at front of work, knit 2, then knit 2 from cable needle, slip next 2 stitches onto cable needle and hold at back of work, knit 2, then knit 2 from cable needle, knit 2.
Row 8: Knit 2, purl 8, knit 2.
These 8 rows set pattern.
Continue in pattern to desired length (to fit around head, mine measured 44cm/17½in), ending with right side facing for next row.
Cast off.

Join cast on and cast off edges to form a loop.

Knitting Journal

Keep track of your projects and any vital information that you may need in the future (always keep a note of your washing instructions - the ball band has this information).

My Project Record

Name of project:

Source of pattern:

Yarn used (name/brand/colour/fibre content)**:**

Needle size:

Gauge:

Date Started:

Date Finished:

Made for:

Comments:

My Project Record

Name of project:

Source of pattern:

Yarn used (name/brand/colour/fibre content):

Needle size:

Gauge:

Date Started:

Date Finished:

Made for:

Comments:

My Project Record

Name of project:

Source of pattern:

Yarn used (name/brand/colour/fibre content):

Needle size:

Gauge:

Date Started:

Date Finished:

Made for:

Comments:

My Project Record

Name of project:

Source of pattern:

Yarn used (name/brand/colour/fibre content):

Needle size:

Gauge:

Date Started:

Date Finished:

Made for:

Comments:

My Project Record

Name of project:

Source of pattern:

Yarn used (name/brand/colour/fibre content):

Needle size:

Gauge:

Date Started:

Date Finished:

Made for:

Comments:

My Project Record

Name of project:

Source of pattern:

Yarn used (name/brand/colour/fibre content):

Needle size:

Gauge:

Date Started:

Date Finished:

Made for:

Comments:

Something That Every Knitter Needs!

'HE APP TO HELP VITH YOUR NITTING!

heck out my new app or iPhone, iPad & iPod.

eaturing the projects hown in this book with asy to follow HD video utorials.

oin the knitting revolution!

esigned & developed by:

Cre@tiveGoo

Information

Tension

This is the size of your knitting. Every knitting pattern will have a tension quoted. This is how many stitches 10cm/4in in width and how many rows 10cm/4in in length to make a square. If your knitting doesn't match this then your finished garment will not measure the correct size. To obtain the correct measurements for your garment you must achieve the tension.

The tension quoted on a ball band is the manufacturer's average. For the manufacturer and designers to produce designs they have to use a tension for you to be able to obtain the measurements quoted. It's fine not to be the average, but you need to know if you meet the average or not. Then you can make the necessary adjustments to obtain the correct measurements.

How to make a Tension Square

First of all look at the tension details in your pattern. For example it might say "20sts and 28 rows to 10cm/4in measured over stocking stitch using 4mm needles". Make sure you use the correct yarn and needles. Cast on at least 4 extra stitches than the tension states (this will give you the true width of all stitches) and work at least 4 extra rows.

Your knitting might be looser or tighter than the tension required, in which case you just need to alter your needle size. Go up one size if you have an extra stitch or two sizes if you have two extra stitches and the reverse if you have fewer stitches.

Choosing Yarn

Choosing yarn, as one of my friends once described "It is like shopping in an adult's sweetie shop". I think this sums it up very well. All the colours and textures, where do you start? Look for the thickness, how chunky do you want your finished garment? Sometimes it's colour that draws you to a yarn or perhaps you have a pattern that requires a specific yarn. Check the washing/care instructions before you buy.

Yarn varies in thickness; there are various descriptions such as DK and 4ply these are examples of standard weights. There are a lot of yarns available that are not standard and it helps to read the ball band to see what the recommended needle size is. This will give you an idea of the approximate thickness. It is best to use the yarn recommended in the pattern.

Keep one ball band from each project so that you have a record of what you have used and most importantly how to care for your garment after it has been completed. Always remember to give the ball band with the garment if it is a gift.

The ball band normally provides you with the average tension and recommended needle sizes for the yarn, this may vary from what has been used in the pattern, always go with the pattern as the designer may change needles to obtain a certain look. The ball band also tells you the name of the yarn and what it is made of, the weight and approximate length of the ball of yarn along with the shade and dye lot numbers. This is important as dye lots can vary, you need to buy your yarn with matching dye lots.

Pressing and Aftercare.

Having spent so long knitting your project it can be a great shame not to look after it properly. Some yarns are suitable for pressing once you have finished to improve the look of the fabric. To find out this information you will need to look on the yarn ball band, where there will be washing and care symbols. Once you have checked to see if your yarn is suitable to be pressed and the knitting is a smooth texture (stocking stitch for example), pin out and place a damp cloth onto the knitted pieces. Hold the steam iron (at the correct temperature) approximately 10cm/4in away from the fabric and steam. Keep the knitted pieces pinned in place until cool.

As a test it is a good idea to wash your tension square in the way you would expect to wash your garment.

Stockist List

AUSTRALIA: Australian Country Spinners, Pty Ltd, Level 7, 409 St. Kilda Road, Melbourne Vic 3004.
Tel: 03 9380 3830
Email: sales@auspinners.com.au

AUSTRIA: Coats Harlander GmbH, Autokader-strasse 31, A -1210 Wien. Tel: (01) 27716 – 0

BELGIUM: Coats Benelux, Ring Oost 14A, Ninove, 9400, Belgium Tel: 0346 35 37 00
Email: sales.coatsninove@coats.com

CANADA: Westminster Fibers Inc, 8 Shelter Drive, Greer South Carolina, NH03060 Tel: 800 445-9276
Email: rowan@westminsterfibers.com

CHINA: Coats Shanghai Ltd, No 9 Building , Baosheng Road, Songjiang Industrial Zone, Shanghai.
Tel: (86- 21) 5774 3733 Email: victor.li@coats.com

DENMARK: Coats Danmark A/S, Nannasgade 28, 2200 Kobenhavn N Tel: (45) 35 86 90 50
Fax: (45) 35 82 15 10 Email: info@hpgruppen.dk
Web: www.hpgruppen.dk

FINLAND: Coats Opti Oy, Ketjutie 3, 04220 Kerava
Tel: (358) 9 274 871

FRANCE: Coats France / Steiner Frères, SAS 100, avenue du Général de Gaulle, 18 500 Mehun-Sur-Yèvre Tel: (33) 02 48 23 12 30
Web: www.coatscrafts.fr

GERMANY: Coats GmbH, Kaiserstrasse 1, D-79341 Kenzingen Tel: (49) 7644 8020
Web: www.coatsgmbh.de

HOLLAND: Coats Benelux, Ring Oost 14A, Ninove, 9400, Belgium Tel: 0346 35 37 00
Email: sales.coatsninove@coats.com

HONG KONG: Coats Shanghai Ltd, No 8 Building, Export & Processing Garden, Songjiang Industrial Zone, Shanghai. Tel: (86- 21) 5774 3733-326
Email: victor.li@coats.com

ICELAND: Storkurinn, Laugavegi 59, 101 Reykjavik
Tel: (354) 551 8258 Email: storkurinn@simnet.is

ISRAEL: Beit Hasidkit, Sokolov St No2, 44256 Kfar Sava Tel: (972) 97482381

ITALY: Coats Cucirini s.r.l., Via Sarca 223, 20126 Milano Tel: 800 992377
Email: servizio.clienti@coats.com

KOREA: Coats Korea Co Ltd, 5F Eyeon B/D, 935-40 Bangbae- Dong, Seocho-Gu, Seoul Tel: (82) 2 521 6262. Web: www.coatskorea.co.kr

LEBANON: y.knot, Saifi Village, Mkhalissiya Street 162, Beirut
Tel: (961) 1 992211 Email: y.knot@cyberia.net.lb

LUXEMBOURG: Bastel Kiste, Rue Du Fort Elizabeth 17-19, 1463 Luxemburg Tel: 00352 40 05 06

MALTA: John Gregory Ltd, 8 Ta'Xbiex Sea Front, Msida MSD 1512, Malta
Tel: +356 2133 0202, Email: raygreg@onvol.net

NEW ZEALAND: ACS New Zealand, 1 March Place, Belfast, Christchurch. Tel: 64-3-323-6665

NORWAY: Coats Knappehuset AS, Pb 100 Ulset, 5873 Bergen. Tel: (47) 55 53 93 00

SINGAPORE: Golden Dragon Store, 101 Upper Cross Street #02-51, People's Park Centre, Singapore 058357. Tel: (65) 6 5358454
Email: gdscraft@hotmail.com

SOUTH AFRICA: Arthur Bales LTD, 62 4th Avenue, Linden 2195 Tel: (27) 11 888 2401
Email: arthurb@new.co.za

SPAIN; Coats Fabra, Santa Adria 20, 08030 Barcelona Tel: 932908400
Email: atencion.clientes@coats.com

SWEDEN: Coats Expotex AB, Division Craft, JA Wettergrensgatta 7, Vastra Frolunda, 431 30 Goteburg Goteborg Tel: (46) 33 720 79 00

SWITZERLAND: Coats Stroppel AG, CH -5300 Turgi (AG) Tel: (41) 562981220

TAIWAN: Cactus Quality Co Ltd, 7FL-2, No 140, Roosevelt Road, Sec 2,Taipei, Taiwan, R.O.C.
Tel: 886-2-23656527 Email: cqcl@m17.hinet.net

THAILAND: Global Wide Trading, 10 Lad Prao Soi 88, Bangkok 10310. Tel: 00 662 933 9019
Email: global.wide@yahoo.com

U.S.A.: Westminster Fibers Inc, 8 Shelter Drive, Greer South Carolina, NH03060.
Tel: 800 445-9276
Email: rowan@westminsterfibers.com

U.K: Rowan, Green Lane Mill, Holmfirth, West Yorkshire, England HD9 2DX.
Tel: +44 (0) 1484 681881 Fax: +44 (0) 1484 687920
Email: mail@knitrowan.com
Web: www.knitrowan.com

Acknowledgements

Many thanks to: - My family and friends for all their support. To the team at Creativegoo especially Darren without whom this could not have happened. Michael Wicks for his stunning photography and patience! Jennifer-Jayne Stone and Charlotte Reynolds for modelling and doing so well in the conditions. Mary Potter, Jane Ashworth and Wendy Shipman for their beautiful knitting, Barbara Farris for her proofreading. Mark Armstrong for his technical contribution and all his support.

Kate Buller and all at Rowan for their support. Sharon Brant for her endless help and support since becoming a freelance designer - thank you for persuading me to take the jump!

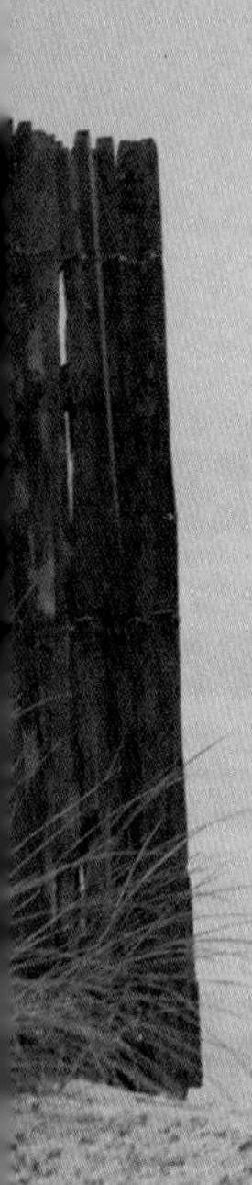